Skurtu, Romania

TARA SKURTU

Skurtu, Romania

EYEWEAR — **AVIATOR**

2016 SERIES

For Hilda —
May you find poetry
and love everywhere you
arrive.
♥ Tara
8. twentyeight. 23.
Brooklyn.

First published in 2016
by Eyewear Publishing Ltd
Suite 333, 19-21 Crawford Street
Marylebone, London W1H 1PJ
United Kingdom

Typeset with graphic design by Edwin Smet
Author and cover photograph by Cătălin Georgescu
Printed in England by Lightning Source
All rights reserved © 2016 Tara Skurtu

The right of Tara Skurtu to be identified as author of this work has been asserted in accordance with section 77 of the Copyright, Designs and Patents Act 1988

ISBN 978-1-911335-47-4

Eyewear wishes to thank Jonathan Wonham for his generous patronage of our press.

WWW.EYEWEARPUBLISHING.COM

TABLE OF CONTENTS

- 9 ȘORICEL
- 10 LIMIT
- 11 VECTOR
- 12 RICHTER SCALE, BUCHAREST
- 14 DESIRE
- 15 BRAINS
- 16 SPOILED
- 17 DERIVATIVES
- 31 LONG POEM, BUCHAREST
- 32 OPERATING SYSTEM
- 33 BAR POEM
- 34 HUNGER
- 36 ECLIPSE
- 37 NIGHT COMMUNION

- 39 ACKNOWLEDGEMENTS

ȘORICEL

The soul is a white mouse
burrowed inside the mouth
of a sleeping child until he yawns.

Easier to leave the soulless boy
asleep than catch the mouse
by its tail.

LIMIT

My body, a strange passenger
surrounded by walls
of books in a language

I don't understand. I'm trying

for sleep in another country.
I'm taking pictures of
pictures of you.

VECTOR

You were everywhere
from all directions pointing
inward to an entry shot

smaller than a pencil
point, graphite visible
between the wrinkles

of my right thumb joint.
– Probably you too will spend
twenty-five years or more

in my body like this
grey speck once housed
in the yellow wood

I held in my left hand
while I tried to slice open
a pear with an adult's knife.

RICHTER SCALE, BUCHAREST

Our first week, you showed me around
your empty capital in a dream. We skipped

Parliament and headed down Calea Victoriei,
lit beeswax candles for the living,

drank jasmine tea at Serendipity, then
a big one hit. I would've asked

what happened next, but I was in it, I knew,
I could feel it: you'd have saved yourself

if it weren't for each day you forget how.
You're like that musicologist I've read about –

seventeen-second memory. Every 3.4
blinks, forgets what he's forked into his mouth,

his daughter's name, his own. Every *I*
he writes, once written, a trick

of someone else's hand. He remembers
composition, and he remembers his wife.

Every time he sees her he's seeing her
for the first time in ten years, and he wants

to waltz. Every time she walks into his room
she steps around a box. I am this wife.

I'm stuck in your village, walking
a chicken on a leash. He pecks the ring of sun-

flower seeds around this house on Lavender Street
– lavender in another language. We're stuck

in November, he and I, waiting for you
to walk into the side yard, past the little black

dog tunneling a lattice of wormholes in the dirt.

DESIRE

That black curl hanging like a fishhook
about your brow – unnoticed until you open
the English-Romanian dictionary
to find the essential verbs,
and as you look down at the page, this helix
of a few strands obscures the spelling
of the translation for *need*.

BRAINS

You didn't have any
that Sunday afternoon
at the family table – your chain-
smoking father, too weak
to tend his backyard garden,
still masculine enough to want
to rip that necklace from your neck,
in silence he slid the first slice
onto my plate and waited for me
to eat the one thing I told myself
I'd never eat – I swallowed
the bite whole. Here, I was
the foreigner. I was your guest.

SPOILED

You don't know how to give
your words to the world this morning,
so you get out of bed, grab a shirt
from the pile of worn shirts, take
a walk to the corner market. I'm listening
to the man in the apartment below sing
ooh don't you wanna take her home,
and you're half asleep picking through
a bin of fruit. You come back to bed
with a perfect apple, put it in my palm.
So small, so red. I can't wait to eat it
alone. I shut the door behind me
in the kitchen and turn on the news.
Two dumbfounded men lean over
the world's new largest loaf
of rustic potato bread, 96.6 kg.
The man below the apartment sings
ooh don't you wanna break her.
I bite the apple and wish
I hadn't – the flesh mealy, a mouthful
of sweet mashed potatoes I spit
into the garbage. The news anchor eyes
the big mound of bread like a trampoline,
the other man pierces it with a serrated knife.
A perfect yeasty line of steam mists
up and out of the screen, warming
this room where I sit holding the world's
most horrible apple, listening to Romanian
Blondie on a loop, and to you, in the shower
down the hall, scrubbing the sweat
of our morning from your skin.

DERIVATIVES

> Romania, 2013–14

I.

It's fall today, was winter last week.
I was happier then, the lined mounds

of raked earth, the potatoes dug up.
In the summer kitchen, a fly zips

into the flytrap. Its body puttied
to the glue strip, legs waving

like six wet strokes of black ink.

In a park by the city wall, you search
out a green-gold leaf in the grass,

unzip my breast pocket, insert
the stem as it starts to rain.

*

*This is the park where new lovers
come to walk,* says a passerby.

This is the park of my childhood,
you tell me in the back of a taxi,

pointing at the green blurring
through the triangular glass.

Love no far, poetry no far,
says the taxi driver two weeks from now.

Fingered into the sidewalk
in a Union Square on the other side

of the world, *I loe you.*

*

You told me you wanted to change
the title of my poem from 'Desire'

to 'Need'. We walked to Cinema City.
You pointed out the neighborhood

cemetery, and I climbed the stone wall
to peek over red-lit rows of glass

rooms and graves. When I reached
the ledge, it crumbled in my grip.

*

– But that poem wasn't about
you. Desire, a blind spot

supplying the vessels of mind
and sight a peripheral view,

and need, this preverbal lump
of a poem I try to unstick,

to unravel while I walk before
the rain to be rained on, thinking

about the Lermontov pin
you never take off, and how

the dueler either shoots up
in the air and gets shot,

or, in the name of honor
or love or spite, aims

for the opponent's left lung.

*

Pushkin never learned, Lermontov
never learned, that the thing to do

is avoid the duel altogether.
I'd quote Pushkin, but I can read

him only in translation:
I want to understand you,

I study your obscure language.
You're so selfish with your fear –

you say man, to thrive, must fall
into a vacuum, must be a bird

inside a vacuum. I've lost
your guilt, and I want it back.

⋆

I couldn't unstick the poem
on my walk in the rain, but when

I reached the market in Berceni,
the curbside cabbages calmed me.

Crenellated pyramids of cabbage,
spring green and veined, each head

stabilizing at least several other heads
like a network of humming, healthy

minds, and the waxy squeak of one
pulled apart from the rest.

⋆

My last night in Bucharest, I leave
the subtitles off. Today I learned

that a baby bird in the care of
human hands needs one worm

per hour. There's a couple
on the TV, naked, in the woods.

The man turns his back to the camera
and urinates into his cupped hands,

shows the woman how to survive
a little longer without water.

⋆

After our embrace in the hotel
lobby, Lermontov leapt

from your lapel and landed face down
on the pink marble. His copper nose

wobbled like a top between
my suitcase and us. You said,

He did it because of the emotion.

We made sure he wasn't damaged,
then you pinned him back.

I thought he did it in the name of
an untranslatable word.

⋆

The news says today is the last day
of spring weather for the year.

Yesterday the moon was out all day
and no one seemed to notice.

I open the dictionary and look up
the word *dictionary*, again –

The poet is a limit, you said.
I thought you were talking calculus:

love, no far: poetry, no far.

II.

Late October, you lay beside me
and I stared at the evil eye

hanging from the bookshelf.
I began to draw it in my notebook –

noted in black what should have been
primary blue, white, baby blue –

and you crossed your legs, your knee
blocking the pupil from my view.

*

Over coffee, I show you how to discover
your dominant eye. All you need

is a sheet of paper with a hole
the size of a pencil eraser.

I hold it in front of you
at arm's length, tell you to look

through, focus on one object
in the near distance. *Close first*

your right eye, then your left.
You don't see a thing.

*

All night you transcribe poems
in the corner bedroom, the door

closed. After ten, I take
a walk down Strada Moldoviţa.

Two churches beside each
other at the end of the street –

one orthodox, a single wooden
cupola, an open gate. The other

evangelical – brick, boarded up,
covered in scaffolding, Xs

in the arches of the bell towers.
On a park bench, I listen

to the strays of Bucharest
calling out, responding –

the only English I hear, in my head.

*

*This feeling continually approaches
a given word, but doesn't*

meet it at any finite distance.

*

Ultimately *you will leave*, you said.

⋆

Last night you edited translations.
You wrote the French word

for love instead of death, realized
your mistake, shook your head.

⋆

The flower pot at your door, full
of dirt and sticks. In your bed

I fold a piece of paper in half,
half, in half again. I cut a crescent

fractal, craft a snowflake
flower, give it the tallest twig

for a stem and stick it in the dirt. It lasts
the night, goes missing by morning.

III.

You gave me three Romanian words
for love, two for missing.

On the train at dusk, I rearrange
magazine cutouts of clauses –

sunt mai aproape, I am
closer; *mai bine să nu*, better

not to – I don't know how
to make a complete sentence.

*

Outside the window, the late summer
corn is beginning to crisp, each

sunflower bent like a burnt match.
Crows scribbling indecipherable

signatures around the crops, around
the stork's nest on the power lines.

I pick one, follow it like one blade
of a ceiling fan until I blink

and it blurs, becomes many crows.

*

In Brașov, a student brings up images.
Why don't you write about emotions?

Perhaps I'm the squirrel that runs
three quarters of the way across the road.

*

*How do you define 'emotional damages'
so I know how to answer the question?*

*

Between villages, five old women sit
side by side beside the paved road, each

selling the same pile of curled yellow fungus.
How would I make the right choice?

From Sibiu to Brașov to Bucharest, memory
out-faiths my will to forget.

Between Bucharest and Brașov, I remember
last night's dream – I sent

you to the hospital. You were allergic
to the food my mother fed you.

*

Some people need their mothers.
Ștefan told me about a Romanian poet

who, after losing his, wedged the butt
of a blade into a wall, and with open

arms, thrust his chest into it over,
over, until he made an object of his body.

When you were a boy, your mother prepared
daily for her funeral. But today is a good day.

*There are no waves. There are only dolphins
in the Black Sea.* You give her a hand-

carved cutting board, and she prepares
a feast for us, shows me black

and white baby pictures of you,
and later, your head in my lap.

*

In bed you once remembered the feeling
of a verse in German, but couldn't explain

it in English. I'd dreamt you and I were beginning
a three-legged race on the shore. Hundreds

of rubber bands rained down at our feet,
and I turned to you and said, *God is good to us.*

⋆

Now my mind does nothing with the hour, says
I must make use of these thoughts of you,

which is like trying to understand a poem –

⋆

*How do you define the question
so I know how to question the damages?*

⋆

Some people have birds in their heads,
but you have every single bird in

the world swirling in yours. A love-
bird nudges himself between

my breasts tonight, stays while I change
the bed sheets, have a coffee, then

another. Now he's asleep, his beak
still, his quick pulse quicker than mine.

⋆

Self-perception, cognitive dissonance,
the idea that a behavior can change

a thought. I think of you.

Self-Perception Theory, Cognitive
Dissonance Theory, the belief

that thoughts migrate toward
an action, behavior will change

my thoughts. I'm not thinking

of you. I've decided to leave
the bird in my shirt.

*

I press the nib, I push out words –
place words, blank words.

*Don't forget to smile across
the ocean* is what you wrote –

but the page can't strip
its cotton ribs of ink,

and between two plates
of glass above my bed,

the green-gold leaf is brown.

LONG POEM, BUCHAREST

I'm the person I was afraid I'd be – a blonde
spider on a park bench, spinneret suspended,

threading diacritics between your teeth
in the name of the etymology

of *need*: of violence and force.

I'm beginning to realize my long poem
may be a person I can't avoid,

a snake in the blade of a lawn mower,
striped segments curling in the air

and slapping onto my thighs
a blood just like mine.

OPERATING SYSTEM

Let me be a line, a word
in the middle of a line
in your poem, conjunction
before I, the suffix
of an action, a single letter
looping the next
to its comma, anything
but a period, any
thing, a number-
four suture, needle
driver, negative
space, wallpaper
of bricks at your head-
board, this fricative
breath – your teeth,
my bottom lip.

BAR POEM

I'm here on the patio, no appetite,
drinking a salty margarita. I feel
my liver, ignore it like last night's
glass of water. I'm tired of writing
you down when I should be writing
poems about place. Dusk hits beyond
the man playing the red accordion
on the corner, and the strays of Iași
bark out a score backed by dissonant
frequencies of the evening bells.
This morning I took a walk and found
a noseless man pumping gypsy love songs
on his accordion. I stared into the holes
of his face and thought about the girl
with the green ribbon around her neck.
Had you read the story backwards,
we might not have lost our heads.
It's late. *What time is it?*
I ask a poet who isn't you.
There's time enough, he says.

HUNGER

I stared at my favorite foods and ate
the words for them. Just yesterday I ate ten
sarmale, a pile of mămăligă cu brânză
și smântână, had room for more. Now
my mind was a mouthful of anaphoras,
and you were a man incapable of natural
love. At your parents' house, your father
forked a piece of crispy fried brain
onto my plate and waited. I rolled
the salty custard around on my tongue
and swallowed. I didn't want to like it –
I liked it. The coffee was sweet, the garden
ungardened, and the dog dug a honeycomb
fractal in the dirt. We stood beneath
the tallest evergreen in the village –
all the birds in the village in this tree.
It was November, outside Bucharest,
but sounded like spring in Boston,
birds in the bamboos outside my window.
Your father drove us back, 101.9
Romantic FM aired songs of loss
in English. We passed a jail, some
plowed fields. We unpacked, sorted
leftovers. I could feel that small bite
of brain acidifying in my stomach.
I wanted to shit it out, be done with it,
didn't want to think about thinking
or feel the thinking inside me. Later,
in a living room of friends, no one
spoke, and you were in charge
of the music: *And you already know,*

you already know how this will end.
My thoughts were thick with rooms.
We went to separate beds. At dawn
I woke to a man in the apartment
below belting out in broken English
the chorus of 'Bad Romance'. Outside
the window, a woman on the fifth floor
shook out an area rug, beat it with a broom.
Your cat came over and sat on my chest.
I lay awake thinking of the brain in my gut,
and repeated a line of verse scribbled
on your bedroom wall: *O how long
it's been since I've seen the sun
glowing above the sun.* You were still
sleeping. You slept well.

ECLIPSE

The bird moved when I moved.
It was like a klonopin, it slept

between my breasts – opened its eyes
only when I peeked inside my shirt

and let in light.

NIGHT COMMUNION

We met at the revolving hotel door. You'd shaved
three weeks of growth while I had three glasses
of wine in the lounge – I was too early, I'd gone
and come back. *You're late*, you said.

I touched your cheek, your neck, your Adam's apple
beading from a slip of the blade. Chanting lured us
diagonally across the street to the Orthodox
evening service. Asters spiraled the pillars.

We stood on the steps behind the crowd. A grievous
a cappella glow, a special ceremony. Men right
beside the women tonight. *Maybe Mary*, you said.
Or a marriage. I thought Jude –

*These be they who separate themselves, sensual,
having not the Spirit.* You tapped my shoulder,
made a quick sign of the cross, and we turned
and ducked away. A shoeless gypsy

baby threw her bottle at your feet. You set it
upright beside her mother, walked on ahead
of me toward an oak growing out of and thick
as the sidewalk. I took a blurry photograph

of you approaching this trunk, and behind you
the painted white arrow on the asphalt pointed
back to where I stood. You'd just walked over it.
Tomorrow I'd be leaving. It wasn't yet late –

I was beginning to dream in your language. You, already too good at mine, afraid of falling. We arrived at a comedy club without a comedy act. The cognac, too sweet. We sat upstairs. I faced the mirror. *Tell me a story*, you said.

ACKNOWLEDGMENTS

Haverthorn: 'Vector'
Memorious: 'Șoricel'
Paper Darts: 'Operating System'
Plume: 'Night Communion,' 'Brains,' 'Paradox,' and 'Eclipse'
Poetry Wales: 'Long Poem, Bucharest'
Redivider: 'Desire' and 'Limit'
spoKe: 'Hunger'
Tahoma Literary Review: 'Derivatives'
The Common: 'Richter Scale, Bucharest' and 'Bar Poem'

Anthologies
The Plume Anthology of Poetry, Volume 4: 'Spoiled'
Vanguard Editions Poetry Anthology #2: 'Vector'

Thanks
First, I'd like to thank the incredible Eyewear Publishing team – especially Todd Swift and Kelly Davio – for giving my poems such a trusted and inviting home. A big, big thank you to the editors of magazines and anthologies where these poems first appeared. (Editors do some of the hardest work in the world for us writers, and without them I wouldn't be where I am, writing this page.)

I also wouldn't be where I am without the following people: my dad (my favorite person in the world) for teaching me how to write and the made-up shape *slibeedoo* – it's because of you I now create my own written shapes from experience; Lloyd Schwartz – my first poetry teacher, always mentor, close friend – for writing all over that first poem until I could barely see the print, for telling me my stupid idea to focus on poetry instead of medicine was a terrific one (and to everyone reading this: I've never met a more precise line-by-line editor of poems); Robert Pinsky – also my always mentor – for working patiently with me poem after poem until I realized I had a collection, for your constant readings, help with order, your never-ending support and advice as I grow on this path; Jill McDonough, for your constant support, for teaching me how to teach poetry like a badass; Louise Glück, for your generosity, for getting me to realize I could write a long poem; Dan Chiasson, for encouraging me to make 'Derivatives' longer; Frank Bidart, for teaching me how to pace a poem with asterisks; Henri Cole, for making me do really strange writing exercises; Gail Mazur; Jericho Brown; Andrea Cohen; Joyce Peseroff; Daniel Lawless; Jenny Barber; Peg and Robert Boyers; Radu Vancu, my Romanian translator and friend; Claudiu Komartin; Florin Iaru, for your enthusiastic support; Cătălin Georgescu, for your beautiful photographs; Caleb Cole; Dan Coman; Duncan Nelson, who asked me to write my first poem, and Elizabeth Alexander, who noticed it and motivated me to keep going. Special thanks to Robert Hildreth for making the Robert Pinsky Global Fellowship in Poetry possible. Your generosity changed my world and my writing – I couldn't have written these poems without it. I'm also grateful for my extended Fulbright in Romania and the Commission staff. And to the lovely people I worked with at Harvard's Edmond J. Safra Center for Ethics. I'm wordlessly grateful for the love and support of my family and friends. Special shout-out to Thomas, Taty (my favorite girl in the world); Amber, Gail (for taking me in as your own), Derek (my poetry partner in crime), Lyza, Abby (you knew before I did!), Tiberiu (my everything partner in crime), Laurențiu, my BU workshop-mates. It's impossible to name everyone. Know that you make this book possible. And so do you readers.

Lightning Source UK Ltd.
Milton Keynes UK
UKOW03f0135100217
293981UK00002B/9/P